Cornelius Star Morehouse

**Ancestry and Descendants of Gershom Morehouse**

Cornelius Star Morehouse

**Ancestry and Descendants of Gershom Morehouse**

ISBN/EAN: 9783337122690

Printed in Europe, USA, Canada, Australia, Japan

Cover: Foto ©ninafisch / pixelio.de

More available books at **www.hansebooks.com**

# Ancestry and Descendants

## of Gershom Morehouse, Jr., of Redding, Connecticut, a Captain in the American Revolution

Compiled
From information furnished by Mr. Nelson D. Adams of Washington, D. C.,
Mr. A. W. Morehouse of Brooklyn, N. Y.,
Mr. Augustus C. Golding of Norwalk, Conn.,
and from town, state and family records.

Printed for private circulation by a descendant of
CAPTAIN GERSHOM MOREHOUSE.

**T**HOMAS MOREHOUSE, the immigrant ancestor, was in Wethersfield,
Conn., as early as 1640. In 1641
he removed to Stamford, and was
one of the original twenty-nine white settlers of
that town who purchased it of the New Haven
Colony, who had previously bought it of the
Indians for one hundred bushels of corn.—*See
New Haven Colonial Records, 1638 to 1649,
pp. 45 and 199.*

In 1653 he settled in Fairfield, and died there in
1658, leaving widow Isabel (who is supposed to
have been a second wife and not mother of his
children) and children Hannah,[2] Samuel[2] (who had
five sons), Thomas,[2] Mary,[2] Jonathan[2] (who married Mary Wilson, daughter of Edward, of Fairfield), and John[2] (who was an ensign in King
Philip's war, 1676, and settled in Southampton,
L. I., where he died October 10, 1701, leaving
children John,[3] Mary,[3] and Phebe[3]).

THOMAS MOREHOUSE,[1] as believed, was. the ancestor of *all* the Morehouses in America; any assertion to the contrary needs confirmation. His name was sometimes spelled in the early records Moorhouse, and at least one branch of his descendants now spell their name Morhous; it is believed that another has adopted the orthography of Morris.

His descendants were found in New Jersey near Newark, Elizabeth, etc., among the old families and settlers, before the Revolution; in Saratoga Co., N. Y., and the northeastern counties of that State; and throughout the west. Those of southwestern Connecticut and of Dutchess and Putnam Counties, New York, are believed to have descended from the son Samuel[1] through his four sons Samuel, Jr.,[2] Thomas,[3] John[1] and Daniel,[3] who married Hannah, daughter of Lieutenant Abraham Adams, of Fairfield, Conn.

1. THOMAS,[1] by the records appears to have purchased in Fairfield on the 6th of August, 1653, twenty-four acres of land on Sasco Hill, a beautiful location near the Sound, and on the

16th day of the same month he purchased of Henry Jackson the first, and for many years the only, grist mill in the town. In September of the same year he was one of the deputies to the General Court at Hartford. He died in August, 1658. His eldest son Samuel² was the executor of his will, and was given a double portion of his property including his houses, barn, mill and mill lot, and other land. His body was probably buried in the southeastern part of the old cemetery in Fairfield.

Samuel and Thomas were made freemen by the General Court, October, 1664.—*Colonial Records, Vol. I.*

In the 1st Book of Record of Stamford is found the following :

The lands & housing now in possession of Thomas Morehouse, and bounded and butted, Viz.: Two dwelling houses, two barns & out houses belonging hereunto with two house lots containing six acres more or less bounded by John Chapman on ye north & Every Sharon on ye south butting ye highway on the west to widows estate. And 8 other peices are described.

3 May 1649.

2.   SAMUEL,[2] son of Thomas,[1] was born as early as 1637, and died 1687 in Fairfield, Conn., and was buried in the old village cemetery; his grave stone bears the oldest date of any yet found in the grounds; it was discovered by Mr. A. W. Morehouse in June 1880, nearly buried in the earth, and by him reset.   He married Rebecca, daughter of William and Rebecca Odell, who came from England to Concord, Mass., in 1639; removed to Southampton, L. I., in 1642, and soon after settled in Fairfield.  Samuel[2] was very often one of a committee appointed by the town to act in the layout of lands and highways.  He was lieutenant of the military company, and the first marshal or sheriff of Fairfield county for some twelve years being removed by order of Sir Edmund Andross.  The records show several grants of land to Samuel[2] from the town, besides one of the "long lots"—which was surveyed back from the village in half mile widths for a distance of twelve miles, with a roadway between each lot, extending north to the highway, now running east and west from Redding Center across Redding Ridge to "Goodrich Hill."  These lots were surveyed by order of the town and at a time when it was feared that the "Crown" would claim all unoccupied land.  Samuel[2] undoubtedly

assisted in the survey, and one of the roads was called the Morehouse road. Their children were: Samuel,[2] Thomas,[2] John,[2] Daniel[2] (born 1678, "Ensign," died May 24, 1739, aged 61), James,[2] Rebecca,[2] Elizabeth,[2] Hannah,[2] Mary,[2] and Ann.[2]

The will of Samuel[1] bears date December 9, 1687, and shows that at that time his sons John, Daniel,[2] and James,[2] were under 20 years of age; and that his daughters Hannah,[2] Mary,[2] and Ann,[2] were under 18; also that Rebecca[2] and Elizabeth[2] had been previously provided for and were, therefore, probably married. In the signature the name is "Sam ll Moorhous."

THOMAS,[2] son of Thomas,[1] married a daughter of Ralph Keeler of Norwalk, by whom he had Jonathan,[3] Thomas,[3] Nathan,[3] Gideon,[3] and Mary;[3] and by Martha, daughter of John Hobby of Greenwich (Jonathan Hobby was an early settler in Greenwich, and this John was probably one of his sons), had son Lemuel, baptized November 1, 1696; in his will gives his wife and son Lemuel all his estate, and says he has given his children by his first wife their full share.

GIDEON,[3] son of Thomas,[2] lived in Fairfield. His wife Mary was probably the person of that name who died in Redding September 13, 1780, mentioned in note on last page of this book; his children were Samuel,[1] Gideon,[4] Zacheus,[1] John,[1] and Abigail.[1]

JOHN,[1] son of Gideon,[3] was of Fairfield; he married, May 16, 1745, Mary, daughter of Edward Jessup, and had Gideon,[5] born December 7, 1746; Edward,[5] born April 13, 1748; Mary,[5] born November 23, 1749; John,[5] born August 25, 1751, and Joseph,[5] born June 11, 1753.

JOSEPH,[5] son of John,[1] was born in Fairfield, married December 19, 1773, Molly, daughter of Talcott Bradley, of Fairfield, and shortly after marriage settled near Ballston Lake in Saratoga Co., N. Y., where he died June 19, 1832; his widow died September 14, 1834, at the same place. He had twelve children, seven sons and five daughters, viz: Joseph,[6] born 1774, John,[6] born 1776, Talcott,[6] born 1778, Molly,[6] born 1780, Jessup,[6] born 1782, Daniel,[6] born 1784, Esther,[6] born 1787, Talcott[6] (2d), born 1789, Bradley,[6] born 1791, Abby,[6] born 1793, Annie,[6] born 1795, and Matilda,[6] born 1797.

JESSUP,[6] son of Joseph,[5] born July 15, 1782, married, February 6, 1806, Ruth, daughter of Deliverence Andrews, of Stillwater, N. Y. He resided in Ballston, Saratoga Co., N. Y. (a farmer), and died there July 19, 1868; his wife died February 9, 1861. His children were: Mary,[3] born 1806, Olivia,[3] born 1808, Joseph D.,[3] born 1810, Esther,[3] born 1813, Hibbard,[3] born 1815, Lory, born 1818, and Harriet A.,[3] born 1821.

Olivia,[3] second daughter of Jessup,[6] was born in Ballston, N. Y., July 23, 1808, married, March 4, 1829, Riley M. Adams, of Bristol, Vt. Her children were: Henry P.,[8] born 1829, died in infancy; Nelson D.,[8] born April 6, 1831, Rebecca,[8] born November 27, 1834, and Catherine B.,[8] born April 27, 1836.

Mr. Nelson D.[8] Adams, above named, now of Washington, D. C., has in course of compilation a Morehouse Family Genealogy, designed to include all branches of the descendants of Thomas,[1] the Fairfield settler.

Mary,[2] daughter of Thomas,[1] is mentioned in the will of her father.

John,[2] son of Thomas,[1] was in Southampton, L. I., in 1683, and left son John,[3] who married and left sons Nathan,[4] Gideon,[4] and John.[4]

JONATHAN,[1] son of Thomas,[1] married Mary, daughter of Edward Wilson, had children Jonathan,[2] born January 1, 1677; Martha,[2] born November 2, 1679.

JONATHAN,[2] son of Thomas,[2] married Rebecca, daughter of John Knowles, April 16, 1690.
Children :

> David,[3] settled in New Jersey.
> Jonathan,[3]—not traced.
> John.[3]
> Joshua,[3]—probably went to New Jersey.
> Mary.[3]
> Tryall.[3]
> Mercy,[3] married David Webster of Stamford.
> Deborah, married Jonathan Sturdevant of Norwalk.

3. JOHN,[3] son of Samuel,[2] was born in Fairfield, and married Ruth, daughter of John, Jr., and Abigail (Lockwood) Barlow. He resided through life in Fairfield and died there in 1727. Children :

> James[4] (1st), born March 21, 16—? (prob. 1697), died young.
> Ruth,[4] born April 21, 1699, baptized May 21, 1704, married —— Marvin.

Stephen,[1] born July 12, 1701,[1] baptized May 21
1704. See below.

Gershom,[1] born November 18, 1703, baptized May
21, 1704. See record.

Elizabeth,[1] born March 24, 1705, baptized March
31, 1706, died in infancy.

Elizabeth,[1] born March 31, 1706, baptized May
16, 1708.

James[1] (2d), baptized March 19, 1709–10, died
unmarried. ?

Abijah,[1] baptized April 27, 1712.

John,[1] Jr., baptized September 19, 1714, married
Mary Stuart, had 8 daughters and 2 sons,
viz: Uriah,[2] born 1739, died 1827 (who married Sarah Wheeler ; his only child was John,[3]
Capt., born 1776, father of the late John G.[4]
of Fairfield, Conn.); and William,[5] born
1749, died 1824, who had sons William,[6] Jr.,
and Stephen.[6]

Ephraim,[1] baptized August 28, 1716.

Ann,[1] baptized November 2, 1718.

James[1] (3d), baptized November 11, 1719.

## His will reads :

"Item to my well beloved son Stephen Morehouse of
Chestnut Ridge land at Chestnut Ridge (Redding), also
the farm he dwells upon that I purchased of Capt. Samuel
Couch, with the house and barn." Also gives him a yoke
of oxen that he now has : to his sons Gershom, Abijah,
John, Ephraim and James the rest of his land to be equally
divided among them, the farm that he had given Gershom

to be accounted for as "part of his portion so that his brothers should be equal with him" ; to his daughter Ruth Murwin (married Thomas Murwin, *now Merwin*), his "bigest silver tankard & twenty pounds in bills of credit besides what I have given her." To his daughter Ann Morehouse his "lesser silver tankard & 150 pounds in bills of credit."

Stephen & Gershom, Executors.

28 March, 1727.


DANIEL,[3] son of Samuel,[4] born 1678, married Hannah, daughter of Lieutenant Abraham Adams. He appears to have been a man of good repute and at times one of a committee in relation to town affairs. His will is dated January 23, 1738-9, and a noncupative will dated April —, 1739. He died May 24, 1739, in sixty-first year. Children :

> Abraham,[5] born in 1700, baptized December 22, 1700.
> Sarah,[5] baptized January 10, 1703.
> Hannah,[5] baptized September 24, 1704.
> Daniel,[5] baptized December 29, 1706.
> Rebecca,[5] baptized February 24, 1712.
> Catharine,[5] baptized August 29, 1714.


ABRAHAM,[5] son of Daniel,[3] married, April 12, 1722, Elizabeth, daughter of Andrew and Elizabeth (Peet) Patterson, who was born January 28, 1701.

He was appointed ensign of the first company, or train band, in Fairfield, by the Assembly in May 1743, and was appointed lieutenant of the same by the Assembly in May 1745, and captain of the same in May 1748. He seems to have been a man of strong character and integrity. His will is dated April 27, 1761. He died May 3, 1761, in his sixty-first year. His widow died before November 21, 1785, administrator of his estate appointed on that date. Children :

> Samuel,⁵ born April 8, 1724.
> Sylvanus,⁵ born December 14, 1725.
> Sarah,⁵ born November 28, 1727.
> Hannah,⁵ born November 18, 1729.
> Daniel,⁵ born April 27, 1732.
> Seth,⁵ born July 8, 1734.
> Reyecca,⁵ born February 20, 1736–7.
> Lois,⁵ born March 27, 1739.
> Andrew,⁵ born July 21, 1740.

SAMUEL,⁵ son of Abraham,⁴ married, July 8, 1741, Ruth, daughter of Nathaniel and Ruth (Adams) Wilson. He seems to have been a man of good standing in society, although not as prominent as some of his ancestors in town affairs; he left a good estate, and had the respect of his townsmen. He died April 5, 1773, in his forty-ninth year. His widow died April 28, 1775, in her fifty-sixth year. His will is dated March 15, 1773. Children:

Lois,⁴ born February 24, 1746.
Isaac,⁴ born August 31, 1749.
Ruth,⁴ born August 15. 1753.
Elizabeth,⁴ born August 15, 1753.
Eunice,⁵ born August 6, 1756.
Abraham,⁶ born March 26, 1758.

ABRAHAM,⁶ son of Samuel,⁵ born March 26, 1758, married, February 17, 1780, Ruth, daughter of Nathaniel and Sarah (Silliman) Wilson, who was born September 14, 1758. He was over six feet in height, of a strong sinewy build, commanding appearance, and was usually called Captain. He, with a companion, was on the beach at Fairfield when the British forces landed and proceeded to burn the town. They hastily notified all they could. The companion was killed and Abraham was captured by the British and taken to New York and put on board the prison ship where he remained until exchanged. He received a pension for many years before his death, which occurred in Fairfield, Conn., September 12, 1841, aged eighty-four years. He lived at ease and enjoyed the comforts of an ample competency for many years, and at his death left a goodly estate to his heirs. His wife died October 30, 1835, aged 77 years. Children :

> Nathaniel,[7] born April 23, 1781.
> Ruth,[ ] born September 1, 1782.
> Sally,[7] born July 4, 1784.
> Joseph,[7] born January 10, 1787.
> Anson,[7] born March 3, 1789.
> Clara,[7] born October 2, 1791.
> Abraham,[7] born December 21, 1800.

ANSON,[7] son of Abraham,[6] married, first, Anne, daughter of Abel and Elizabeth (Halleck) Treadwell, in the spring of 1810, who died April 11, 1823. Children :

> Lorinthe,[ ] born August 17, 1811.
> Albert,[ ] born March 14, 1814.

He married second, Sally, daughter of William and Hannah (Bulkley) Jennings, December 14, 1823. One child :

> Abraham W.,[ ] born April 23, 1828.

In May 1836 he removed to Royalton, Niagara Co., N. Y. He was a farmer as were all of his paternal ancestors. He was a man of excellent intellectual faculties, good judgment, decided opinions, respected by all who knew him for his kindness, justice, and conscientiousness. He was quick in his movements, of marvelous strength, and great self-control. He died in Royalton, Niagara Co., N. Y., March 27, 1847. His widow died in Bridgeport, Fairfield Co., Conn., August 4, 1884. She was born May 2, 1799.

ABRAHAM W.,[2] son of Anson,[1] born April 23, 1828, married, August 17, 1856, Mary J., daughter of James Benj. and Maria (Brothwell) Wilson, who was born May 22, 1837. Children:

> Melvin W.,[3] born December 23, 1862.
> Leonard B.,[3] born September 26, 1865.
> Emma,[3] born July 7, 1868.

MELVIN W.,[3] son of Abraham W.,[2] unmarried. A machinist, engineer and mechanical expert, now (July 1894) in Sydney, Australia. Left New York February 10, 1894, under a contract for six months to start the initial plant of Mergenthaler Linotype Machines in that country. He has a wide experience and has been uniformly successful in business; has held positions of trust and responsibility, and has won the confidence and esteem of all.

LEONARD BANGS,[3] son of Abraham W.,[2] born September 26, 1865, married, June 27, 1888, Edith May, daughter of John H. and Nancy J. (Raymond) Kedney, who was born February 17, 1860. He was early employed by a leading firm in Bridgeport, Conn., then assistant secretary of the Young Men's Christian Association, after that employed in a large mercantile house in New York City, and now manager and in charge of a manufacturing business. Children:

Helen Claire,[1] born November 17, 1890.
Raymond Irving,[1] born January 8, 1892.

Emma,[3] daughter of Abraham W.,[2] born July 7, 1868, married, September 11, 1888, Rev. C. A. Shatto, of Trumbull Co., Ohio, and died February 8, 1892, in Brooklyn, N. Y.; buried in Greenwood Cemetery. No children.

STEPHEN,[1] son of John,[3] was born in Fairfield July 12, 1701, baptized May 21, 1704, married March 21, 1722, Abigail, daughter of John and Abigail (Minor) Tredwell, born October 7, 1702, died September 5, 1759, in her fifty-sixth year. He settled in Redding, Conn., and is said to have been the founder of the Episcopal parish in that town. He died May 2, 1767, "in ye 66 year of of his age," and was buried in the Episcopal

church yard on Redding Ridge.   His tombstone
is still standing.   His wife died September 6, 1759,
in her fifty-sixth year.   Children :

> Joseph,⁵ born February 17, 1724.
> Daniel,⁵ born July 21, 1726.
> Elizabeth,⁵ born November 1, 1728.
> Abigail,⁵ born May 8, 1731.
> Stephen,⁵ Jr., born September 25, 1733.   See
>     below.
> Ann,⁵ born December 15, 1737.
> John,⁵ born December 15, 1739, settled in Ridge-
>     field, Conn.
> Abel,⁵ born July 15, 1741.

On pages 54 and 55, Beardsley's *History of the
Episcopal Church in Connecticut*, it reads that in
"October, 1722, fourteen subscribers in Newtown,
including one from Woodbury and one from
Chestnut Ridge (Redding), returned their thanks,
etc., and requested the Honorable Society to send
them a lawfully ordained Minister."   Probably
the one from Chestnut Ridge was Stephen Morehouse.   Again, on page 68, that the Rev. Mr.
Caner of Fairfield says he preached or lectured
once in three weeks to about twenty families at
Chestnut Ridge (Redding).   On page 173 "that
a second and larger church had been built at Redding in 1750."

STEPHEN,[3] JR., son of Stephen,[1] was born September 25, 1733, married, 1st, April 8, 1759, Sarah Hawley, of Newtown, Conn., who died March 28, 1776, aged 41. He married, 2d, October 3, 1779, Anna Stiles of Lanesboro, Vt., who died March 31, 1805, aged 60. He settled in early life in New Preston, Conn., and died there in 1817, aged 84. Children by 1st wife:

Benjamin,[4] born April 21, 1760. See below.
Stephen,[4] born March 8, 1762.
Sarah,[4] born April 21, 1764.
Rhoda,[4] born October 31, 1766.
Olive,[4] born December 6, 1768.
Hannah,[4] born May 9, 1772.
Ruth,[4] born March 27, 1774.

By 2d wife:

Stiles,[4] born April 15, 1783.
Augustine,[4] born September 20, 1785.

BENJAMIN,[6] son of Stephen,[3] was born April 21, 1760, in New Milford, Conn., and in early life settled in Washington, Conn., where he married, November 3, 1786, Jane Hill. He died in Washington May 6, 1846, aged 86, his wife having died in 1830.

Children :

> Hawley,[7] born August 1, 1788 ; married, January
> 28, 1811, Betsey Marsh.  He died August —,
> 1846.
>
> Dimon,[7] born April 2, 1790 : married, February 3,
> 1817, Huldah Titus ; he died March 28, 1846,
> aged 58.  He was the father of Hon. Henry
> H.[7] Morehouse, who for many years has been
> Judge of Probate of the Washington District.
>
> Sarah,[7] born July 6, 1791.
>
> Polly,[7] born November 27, 1792.
>
> Alba,[7] born April 13, 1794.
>
> Leman,[7] born January 17, 1796, died September
> —, 1838.
>
> Seymour,[7] born January 24, 1798.

STEPHEN,[6] son of Stephen,[5] settled in Amenia,
N. Y., died there, and was buried in Sharon, Conn.
His son Salmon[7] (born January 27, 1789, died July
1, 1841), of New Milford, had daughter Sarah,[7]
born 1826, who married Noble G. Bennitt of New
Milford, whose son, Rev. George Stephen Bennitt
is Rector of Grace Church, Jersey City, N. J.

For a fuller record of this branch of the family
see *History of New Milford, pages 732–737.*

4. GERSHOM, SR.,[1] son of John, was born November 18, 1703. He married Sarah, daughter of John Hill, April 22, 1725. To them was born a son Gershom,[5] November 25, 1727, and a daughter Elizabeth,[5] January 3, 1730. Ruth[5] was born December 23, 1733. Evidently the family removed to Redding in 1737. He and his wife were admitted as members of the Redding church May 8, 1737, "on recommendation of Rev. Mr. Hobart of Fairfield."

5. GERSHOM, JR.,[5] son of Gershom, Sr.,[1] was born November 25, 1727, and married Anna Sanford January 18, 1748, who survived him many years and died, as it reads on her tombstone, July 27, 1822, aged 90 years and 6 months.

Gershom, Jr.,[5] entered the Revolutionary army as a private, was appointed 1st Lieutenant 1st Conn. Battalion March 15, 1777, and afterward promoted Captain. He was in command of a company at the battle of White Plains. His son-in-law, a Captain in the British troops, was in the same battle, and they were permitted to meet after the action, under a flag of truce, to confer on family matters.

Thomas Sanford, an American loyalist, was a Captain of Cavalry in the "British Legion" during the Revolutionary war.—*See Sabine's American Loyalists.*

He married Tabitha[6] daughter of Gershom[3] and removed with his family to Montreal at the close of the war, where he was afterward accidentally drowned. He is supposed to have received a pension from the British government. It is believed that descendants of Capt. Sanford are still residing in Montreal.

Gershom, Jr.,[5] died in Redding, January 22, 1805, aged 77 years. His tombstone, as well as that of his wife, may be seen in excellent condition in the old unused burial ground just west of the Congregational church in Redding.

The children of Gershom, Jr.,[5] and Anna Sanford were:

Ezra,[6] baptized April 28, 1754.
Billy,[6] baptized July 18, 1756.
Aaron,[6] baptized June 4, 1758.
Jane,[6] baptized November 4, 1760.
Anna,[6] baptized June 19, 1764.
Hill,[6] baptized May 5, 1765.
Lucy,[6] baptized July 12, 1767.
Betty,[6] baptized August 6, 1769.
Elizabeth Ruth,[6] baptized November 10, 1771.
Polly,[6] baptized May 15, 1774.
Tabitha,[6] no record of baptism.

Owing to the fact that the records of the Episcopal Church in Redding, previous to 1833, have been lost, the records of the Morehouses of this generation are necessarily incomplete. The facts must be chiefly gained from other sources. Sabine's "American Loyalists," and the will of Gershom' throw some light on the matter.

In Sabine's "*American Loyalists of the Revolution*" mention is made of three Morehouses as follows:

(1) "Morehouse, Daniel, of Connecticut, a member of the Reading Association. He became an officer in the Queen's Rangers, and retired at the close of the war on half pay. He went to New Brunswick and was a magistrate and major in the militia. He died in the County of York in 1835, aged 77."

(2) "Morehouse, James. A grantee of St. John, New Brunswick, in 1783."

(3) "Morehouse, John, of Connecticut, a member of the Reading Association. He settled in Nova Scotia and at his decease was one of the oldest magistrates in the Colony. He died on Digby Neck in 1839, aged 78."

It appears that "Reading Association" was an association in Redding who were pledged "to defend, maintain and preserve, at the risk of their lives and property, the prerogatives of the crown and the privileges of the subjects, from the attacks of any rebellious body of men, any Committees of Inspection, of Correspondence," etc.

It is difficult to identify either of the parties named with certainty, though it seems probable that as Daniel and John were members of the Association that they must have resided in or near Redding. As Daniel died in 1835, aged 77, he must have been born about 1758, and by the same process it is found that John was born about 1751, probably, therefore, they were of the same generation as the children of Capt. Gershom,³ and *may* have been sons of one of his brothers.

Descendants of John Morehouse are very numerous in and about Digby, Nova Scotia, and are represented as being very worthy people, noted for honesty and morality.

Stephen,¹ brother of Gershom, Sr.,¹ as appears, "was founder of the Episcopal parish in Redding," and as many of the Episcopalians of the Revolution were loyal to the crown, it seems probable that Stephen's family must have been brought up in that faith, and that the Daniel and John mentioned may have been his grandsons.

The will of Gershom,³ dated in 1799 and admitted to probate 1805, names Billy and Aaron Morehouse as executors. Besides his wife and the two above mentioned, the following legatees are named: Tabby Sanford,⁶ Jane Osborne,⁶ Lucy Morgan,⁶ Elizabeth Ruth Goodsell,⁶ Polly Barnum⁶ and

Daniel,[5] son of Anne[6] Morehouse deceased. The will can be seen at the probate records in Danbury, Conn.

Tabitha,[6] daughter of Gershom, Jr.,[5] married Captain Sanford (see page 24).

Lucy[6] daughter of Gershom, Jr.,[5] married Charles Morgan, farmer, of Hartwick, near Cooperstown, N. Y.

Elizabeth Ruth,[6] daughter of Gershom, Jr.,[5] married —— Goodsell, a blacksmith and store keeper near Cooperstown, N. Y.

Polly[6] (Barnum)—daughter of Gershom, Jr.,[5] record lacking (see will).

Anna,[6] daughter of Gershom[5]—records lacking (see will), but it is supposed that hers was one of the families which removed to Canada at the close of the Revolutionary war. It is known that her son Daniel,[5] after his mother's death came to Connecticut and had a home with his grandparents and afterwards with Aaron.[6]

BILLY,[6] son of Gershom, Jr.,[5] had a family and resided in the west part of Redding. His children were:

Peter,[7] married to Ruth Osborn ; their home was in Ridgefield, Conn.

Aaron,[7] married —— Godfrey, and resided in Poughkeepsie, N. Y.

Ruth,[7] married Thomas Olmstead ; lived in the west part of Redding.

Tabitha,[7] married —— Sanford, and lived near the pond in the west side of Redding.

6.  AARON,[6] son of Gershom, Jr.,[5] was born June 2, 1759, died December 3, 1833.  His tombstone, and that of his wife, is standing in good order in the ancient ground of the Episcopal church in Redding, Conn.  He married Urana Starr (daughter of John Starr, as see history of the Starr family, No. 450, on page 306), who was born November 4, 1768, and died May 2, 1830. Their children were: Starr Hill,[7] Flora,[7] Betsey,[7] Anna,[7] William,[7] Almira,[7] Charles,[7] Amelia,[7] and George.[7]

Aaron,[6] entered the Connecticut Army of the Revolution at the age of sixteen, as Fifer.  He was in the battle of Flatbush, L. I., Red Hook, and other places, and was in the regiment which covered the retreat from New York City.  He received a pension from the U. S. Government the last few years of his life.  His home was in Redding Center, where he cultivated a large farm, and for thirty years was a Deputy Sheriff of Fairfield County; an office of much note, responsibility, and honor in his day.

DANIEL[7] (see will of Gershom[1]), nephew and adopted son of Aaron,[6] on page 33.

STARR HILL,[7] son of Aaron,[6] born January 29, 1788, married —— Fairchild. He died in Redding, and was the father of Anson,[8] Louisa,[8] and Amanda,[8] who all removed to —— New York State, where Anson[8] died in middle life, a bachelor.

Flora,[7] daughter of Aaron,[6] born November 19, 1789, married Bradley Sherwood of Redding—no children. Her second husband was Jeremiah Beers, and they resided in Newtown. He was a large farmer and quite a mechanic. He, with Charles,[7] constructed the first water works in the city of Bridgeport, laying wooden pipes and taking the water from springs on "Golden Hill"—probably the first city water works constructed in Connecticut. They had two children, John and Julius Starr —John died in boyhood and Julius' death was recorded during the past year.

Betsey,[7] daughter of Aaron,[6] born January 11, 1793, married Isaac Sherman, Monroe, Conn.; no children.

Anna,[7] daughter of Aaron,[6] born May 13, 1795, married Nathaniel Sherman, of Monroe, Conn. Children: Flora,[8] wife of Stephen Mallett, a wealthy farmer, now residing at Quaker Farms, Oxford, Conn.; no children. Caroline,[8] and Isabell,[8] both deceased.

WILLIAM,[7] son of Aaron,[6] born April 25, 1797; unmarried; buried at Redding.

Almira,[7] daughter of Aaron,[6] born September 6, 1800; married Nelson Sherman, of Monroe, Conn. Three brothers married three sisters. Children, George Henry[8] died in early youth, Polly Betsey[8] married John Parmelee and resides in Hattertown, southern part of Newtown, Conn.; one son.

7. CHARLES,[7] son of Aaron,[6] born December 13, 1802, still living in Newtown, Conn., aged 91 years; married Fidelia Starr, born January 28, 1800, died August 17, 1833, daughter of Edward Starr (*see Starr book, No. 453, page 309*). He had a great fondness for mechanical work, and was an expert in a remarkable degree in the use of tools. He resided in New Haven, Conn., for many

years. A strong Whig in politics until the war came, and since then an unyielding Republican, and always, from early youth, a staunch Churchman. He married, for his second wife, Anna Morehouse,⁴ daughter of Daniel,⁵ grandson of Gershom,⁶ and Sarah Peck. The children of Charles⁷ and Fidelia Starr: Julia,⁸ died in infancy, Cornelius Starr,⁸ and Fidelia Starr.⁸

8. CORNELIUS STARR,⁸ son of Charles,⁷ born in Redding, January 2, 1830. Has resided in New Haven since 1837. He chose for his life-work the occupation of a printer, and has been in the book-printing business since March 8, 1851. The firm name is now, July, 1894, and has been since September, 1859, Tuttle, Morehouse & Taylor. He married, December 1, 1852, Eliza Kimberly, born January 19, 1832, in West Haven, Conn., the daughter of William Kimberly and Ruth Ann Nichols, granddaughter of Eli and Sarah (Lyon) Nichols of Redding. Eliza Kimberly is a direct descendant of Thomas Kimberly of London, who settled in New Haven 1638, and afterward removed to Stratford, where he died in 1673. His son Eleazur was the first male child born in New Haven, and was for many years Secretary of State.

Mary Louise,⁹ the only child of Cornelius Starr and Eliza Kimberly, born July 19, 1856, married May 4, 1880, to Rev. Edwin Stevens Lines, for the past fourteen years Rector of St. Paul's Episcopal Church, New Haven, Conn. Children:

> Edwin Morehouse,¹⁰ born November 2, 1881.
> Henry Starr,¹⁰ born August 15, 1883, died April 23, 1889.
> Margarett Kimberley,¹ born November 21, 1887, died April 29, 1889.
> Harold Stevens,¹⁰ born March 15, 1889.

Fidelia Starr,⁹ daughter of Charles,² born at Newtown, Conn., August 2, 1833; married Edward C. Beecher, of New Haven, Conn., January 28, 1857; died in Pasadena, Cal., October 2, 1891. Their children were:

> Charles Edward,⁹ born July 27, 1859.
> Harriet Woodward,⁹ born September 13, 1861, died August 19, 1863.
> Susie Starr,⁹ born November 14, 1864.
> Henry Nicholson,⁹ born June 28, 1867.
> Anne Fassett,⁹ born December 12, 1872, died March 2, 1892.

Amelia,[7] daughter of Aaron,[6] born September 26, 1805, married Jedediah Adams, of Redding, and resided in Monroe.   Children :

> Mary C.,[*] married John Smith, son of U. S. Senator Perry Smith, of New Milford.
> Anna Maria,[*] married George Gray, of Monroe.


GEORGE,[7] son of Aaron,[6] born March 2, 1812, died July 21, 1886, married Caroline, daughter of Abraham Johnson, January 17, 1832; she was born October 21, 1814, died December 18, 1893.   Children :

> Caroline A.,[*] born August 25, 1833, married Benjamin Crofut November 10, 1850.   One son, George B., born October 20, 1864, resides in Orange, N. J.
> Emily J.,[*] born September 7, 1840, married James M. Smith December 3, 1860.   One child, Nellie D., born September 17, 1862 ; married Horace Walker December 3, 1884 ; one child, Helen, born October 25, 1885.


DANIEL,[7] nephew and adopted son of Aaron.[6] Evidently from tradition, his earliest years were spent in Canada.   He is the only one known to have returned, of those of the family who removed to Canada at the close of the Revolutionary war.

He married, first, Sarah Peck, daughter of Nathan and Huldah (Fabrique) Peck. Sarah died January 6, 1824. Children :

Anna,* born March 7, 1804, married Charles Morehouse,' son of Aaron,* May 31, 1834, died January 28, 1890.

Louis Peck,* born August 4, 1810, married Harriet Augusta Brown, May 18, 1834, died November 9, 1886.

Eliza Jane,' born August 4, 1810, married Charles Fairman, June 18, 1832, died May 21, 1885.

John Beers,* born October 14, 1812, married Laura Ann Osborn, of Monroe, Conn., January 23, 1834, died at Trenton, N. C., January 14, 1845. Had daughter, Ann Jane,* born May 28, 1836, who married Arthur C. Sloat June 11, 1868, at Jefferson, Ashtabula Co., O. Resided in Rushville, Ill., September 29, 1874. No children. Laura Ann Osborn married second time, November 24, 1869, John Ruth, who died January 27, 1880.

Mary,* born June 3, 1815, married James E. Briggs September 15, 1842, died August 1, 1843. Had son Oliver.*

Sarah,* born May 16, 1819, married, first, James E. Briggs, 1844; second, Josiah Booth, October, 1855, died ——.

DANIEL,[7] married second wife, Lucy Thomas; she died August 31, 1832. Children:

> Frank,[ ] born January 7, 1826, died November 20, 1826.
>
> Margaret E.,[ ] born November 27, 1827, married Theodore Parmelee September 28, 1852, died August 31. 1853.
>
> Catharine,[ ] born December 23, 1828, married John Boyer December 30, 1852. Resides in Oconomowoc, Wis.
>
> Frank T.,[ ] born January 23, 1830, married Catharine Boyer November 10, 1851. Resides in Oconomowoc, Wis.

1199550

DANIEL,[7] married third wife, Anna Booth, ——, 1833, died ——. Daniel[7] died May 25, 1840.

LOUIS PECK,[ ] son of Daniel,[7] born August 4, 1810, married, May 18, 1834, Harriet Augusta Brown, daughter of Jabez Brown, 2d, and Catharine Lord; died November 9, 1886. He was a sign and ornamental painter of much note; his home was always in New Haven, Conn. Harriet Brown was a direct descendant of Francis Brown who was one of the prospecting company which came with Governor Eaton to Quinnipiac in advance of the colony, and was one of the seven men who were left to spend the winter of 1637-8 in the hut erected near what is now the corner of Church and George streets. She was born January 24, 1812; died May 12, 1884. Children:

LOUIS PECK Jr.,[9] son of Louis Peck[5] and Harriet (Brown), resides in Chicago, Ill. Born March 30, 1835, married, October 15, 1861, Fredrika Gerhardt, October 15, 1861. He is a graduate of the Sheffield Scientific School of Yale University, of the class of 1856, and has been connected with the Illinois Central Railroad Company for many years as assistant engineer, assistant chief engineer, land commissioner and tax commissioner. Children:

> Clara,[10] born July 16, 1862.
> George Gerhardt,[10] born January 25, 1868.
> Frederick Ballard,[10] born May 14, 1873

Harriet Brown,[9] daughter of Louis Peck[5] and Harriet (Brown), born August 23, 1838, married, May 29, 1862, Ezra Leander Brainerd (Yale College 1859), son of Heber and Esther Hubbard Brainerd. Resides in Chicago, Ill. Children:

> Henry Hamilton,[10] born May 28, 1863.
> William Lord,[10] born January 27, 1865.
> Frederic Hubbard,[10] born August 7, 1866.
> Wallace Heber,[10] born May 14, 1868.

HENRY LOVELL,[9] son of Louis Peck[7] and Harriet (Brown), resides in Chicago, Ill. Born March 2, 1851, married Annie Huebel. Children:

> Albert,[10] born February 15, 1880.
> Herbert,[10] born November 23, 1881.
> Robert,[10] born February 10, 1885, died August 3, 1890.
> Richard,[10] born October 7, 1887.
> Eugene,[10] born November 19, 1889.
> Florence,[10] born February 29, 1892.

Georgia Lord,[9] daughter of Louis Peck[7] and Harriet (Brown), born April 22, 1854, married May 6, 1872, George Ellsworth Maltby, son of George Williams Maltby and Sarah Bogart (a direct descendant of Anneke Jans and Dominie Everhardus Bogardus, the first regular minister of New Amsterdam). Children:

> Maude Evelyn Townshend,[10] born September 9, 1873.
> Dorothy Lord[10] (May Violet), born May 16, 1877.

Jennie,[9] daughter of Louis Peck[7] and Harriet (Brown), born September 23, 1858, died September 3, 1864.

Eliza Jane,[3] daughter of Daniel,[2] born August 4, 1810, died May 31, 1885. Married Charles Fairman June 18, 1832, born November 8, 1809, died December 31, 1886. Children:

Franklin Fairman,[9] born June 22, 1833, married Mary J. Sherman November 30, 1871. Children:

> Matilda Louise,[1] born February 2, 1873.
> Frank Sherman,[1] born August 31, 1875.
> Marion,[1] born March 17, 1879.

Matilda Eliza Fairman,[9] born January 4, 1835, died February 15, 1837.

Daniel Beach Fairman,[9] born May 2, 1836, died February 20, 1837.

Daniel Beach Fairman,[9] born January 11, 1839, married Lucinda L. Southwick October 20, 1860. Children:

> Charles Chauncey[10] born July 22, 1861, married Sarah Overman June 25, 1885. Children:
>
> Ruth,[11] born March 8, 1886.
> Helen,[11] born Nov. 22, 1888, died July, 1892.
> Hazel,[11] born November 26, 1890.
> Charles Chauncey,[11] Jr., born Dec. 27, 1893.
>
> Clarence,[10] born February 2, 1863, married Margaret Miller, January 6, 1887. Child:
>
> Daniel Beach,[11] born August 27, 1890.

Matilda Fairman,[9] born February 1, 1841, died January 23, 1872; married James J. Noble August 18, 1864. Child:

> Mary Eliza,[10] born May 30, 1868.

James Fairman,[9] born March 20, 1843, died January 5, 1870.

Jane Fairman,[9] born March 20, 1843. Auditing Department Illinois Central R. R., Chicago, Ill.

Arthur Fairman,[9] born April 24, 1845, married Sophie B. Seibert, August 31, 1876. Children:

> Charles Edward,[10] born 6, 1877.
> Annie,[10] born December 12, 1878.
> Margarite,[10] born September 7, 1881.
> Arthur,[10] born May 10, 1885.
> Jennie,[10] born February 10, 1891.

Elizabeth Fairman,[9] born April 3, 1848, died Nov. 18, 1874; married George W. Patten Nov. 28, 1872.

Annie Fairman,[9] born August 21, 1849, died December 20, 1886.

Eva Fairman,[9] born November 2, 1851, married James J. Noble August 24, 1875. Child:

> Alden Charles,[10] born May 17, 1880.

Drusius Fairman,[9] born July 6, 1853, died April 11, 1871.

In the old Episcopal church yard on Redding Ridge are stones marked as follows:

Here lies Mr. Zacheus Morehouse
who exchanged this life for immortality
Oct. 4, 1780, in the 69 year of his age.

---

In memory of Mrs. Mary,
widow of Mr. Gideon Morehouse of Fairfield, who died at Redding,
Sept. 13, 1780, aged upwards of 90 years.

The Fairfield Probate Records, Vol. 1754-57. pp. 116-17, show that Gideon Morehouse and wife Abigal had children, Abigal wife of John Lockwood, and sons Samuel, *Zacheus*, *Gideon* and John.

Mr. Nelson D. Adams, 732 7th Street, N. E., Washington, D. C. (maternally of the Morehouse family), is collecting records and facts with a view to the publication of an extensive genealogy of the descendants of Thomas Morehouse, and solicits correspondence with all who may be interested.

Mr. Adams will be greatly aided by Mr. Abraham W. Morehouse, No. 420 Tenth street, Brooklyn, N. Y. (late of Bridgeport, Conn.), and his collections from town and church records.

Members of the Morehouse family can obtain copies of this little book by sending their address and return postage to either of the above named gentlemen.

It is the hope of the publisher that his imperfect work may stimulate an interest among the descendants of the immigrant ancestor THOMAS, and aid in soon publishing a full and complete history of the family.

PRESS OF TUTTLE, MOREHOUSE & TAYLOR, NEW HAVEN, CONN

www.ingramcontent.com/pod-product-compliance
Lightning Source LLC
Chambersburg PA
CBHW030911260626
47169CB00008B/2793